A HUNDRED FLOWERS TO AWARENESS AND DEATH

A Hundred Flowers to Awareness and Death

DR. MOHAN PRASAD JOSHI

Tara
Publishing

A Hundred Flowers to Awareness and Death
(An Anthology of Poems)
Copyright © 2025 by Dr. Mohan Prasad Joshi, MD, MSc, MBBS
All rights reserved. No part of this book may be reproduced in any manner whatsoever without written permission except in the case of brief quotations embodied in critical articles and reviews.
First Printing (US Edition), 2025

Cover background photo credit: Dr. Mohan Prasad Joshi
Drawing credit (page 116 on the print version): Times Creation

To my dad—Professor Dr. Tara Prasad Joshi—who now lives in the stars.

PRAISE FOR A HUNDRED FLOWERS TO AWARENESS & DEATH

In "A Hundred Flowers to Awareness and Death," Poet Joshi navigates the metaphysical terrain of existence, weaving words that untie the secrets to our life's impermanence. This poignant collection takes the readers on a sanctified journey in understanding life and death. Using simple words, the poet explores the verses about the profound awareness of mortality. Each poem mediates the momentary nature of time, urging us to appreciate the beauty of fleeting moments. It precisely explores the interplay between light and darkness, capturing the essence of a life well-lived and the profound contemplation that precedes the inevitable farewell. The poems are not a lamentation but a celebration of life.

- Nabin K Chhetri, M.St in Creative Writing (Oxford University), M.Litt in The Novel (University of Aberdeen), Scottish-Nepalese poet and writer; recipient of awards from Canada, Australia, Italy, India, Nepal, the U.K., U.S. and Israel.

Writing poetry is not detailing an existing fact; instead, it is to create a new reality, a novel outlook, or a perspective on life, existence, and the world. It is ever a journey to novelty—all actions of recreating images, putting one's visions and images into artwork. That is where Dr. Joshi has achieved great success. Every poem is so tremendous and so touching and piercing, like a sharp arrow. Poet Joshi is always optimistic; his poems bear the witness of a person gifted with the unique faculty of imagination required of a creative artist. Dr. Joshi's poems combine intellect, long experience, and a balance of emotion. In his mind sits the elemental question of the cosmos, creation, and the cosmic dancer hidden from the bare eyes. He tries to unravel this mystery from his perspective—in the light of spiritualism, forms change; however, the essence remains imperishable. As he proclaims in one of his poems, the goal of creation will be the experience of suffering, search, and solution. It is genuinely so. The last creation—One flower to awareness and one to death—is a titular poem. It sings the ultimate song of life and death.

- *Govinda Raj Bhattarai, PhD, retired professor of English, Tribhuvan University, Kathmandu; novelist; essayist; literary critic; linguist; translator*

In *A Hundred Flowers to Awareness and Death*, Mohan Joshi wrestles with what it is to be alive, what it is to face death. These poems span the gamut from playful to devastated, philosophical to practical, all of them steeped in curiosity. A beautiful collection—on that invites us, too, to "wake up … as a new flower."

- *Rosemerry Wahtola Trommer, MA in English Language & Linguistics (UW-Madison), author of 13 collections of poetry, including* All the Honey; *host of* The Poetic Path; *winner of several poetry prizes*

Mohan Joshi's *A Hundred Flowers to Awareness and Death* is a window into his life as a matured and awakened man. He sees meaning in everyday activities, such as walking, observing the fall of a leaf, a raindrop, such things bringing an awareness of birth and death, becoming an overarching theme that runs through his poems, a single thread that ties them together.

– *Deepak Shimkhada, PhD, Nepalese-American Educator; professor of Asian Art and Religion, Claremont, California; artist; art historian; author*

A Hundred Flowers to Awareness and Death is a collection of poems that reveal the poet's consciousness to self, soul, Super Soul, life, death, the Earth, and environment. These poems show the eter-

nality of the soul. The protagonist seeks union with the Super Soul in humility. Death is not fearsome but a reminder of the essence of life. The poems, in simple language through spruce images, manifest the poet's quest to merge with all and be part of the cosmos.
 - Dr. DC Chambial, *Indian English poet and critic; editor of Poetcrit; recipient of several awards and honors*

A Hundred Flowers to Awareness and Death represents subtle colors and shades of human experience with precision and power. The collection is full of poetic insights and epiphanic illuminations concerning life, death, beauty, and impermanence, among other aspects of being and becoming. Above all, it is about a perpetual quest for formless awareness that is the source of numerous forms and manifestations of life. The diction of the poems is simple yet effective, and the overall mood meditative, almost spiritual. I feel certain that the aesthetic beauty and humanistic sagacity of the 'hundred flowers' will receive appreciation and love from many readers over a long period of time.
 – Sanjeev Uprety, *PhD, writer, theatre actor, and professor of English, Tribhuvan University, Kathmandu*

A Hundred Flowers to Awareness and Death is a collection of perceptive poems on consciousness and life and death. A strain of melancholy runs through most of the poems, but the suggestive diction and the deeply meditative tone give the reader an intense vision of the nature of things. A powerful work of creative imagination, this anthology takes some of the most common objects and events and transforms them into something uncommonly rich and powerful. It is a silent joy to read these poems and feel a sense of calmness and serenity.
 – Shreedhar Lohani, *PhD, former professor of English, Tribhuvan University, Kathmandu; writer; critic; poet*

Mohan Joshi's poems celebrate the various modes and moments of life. The motifs of the poems are diverse. They capture various serendipitous moments the poet experienced. The poems celebrate diversity and fluidity encountered at different moments of life. I appreciate Joshi's sense of rhythm and his use of the English language in this collection of poems.

– *Abhi Subedi, PhD, professor of English, Tribhuvan University, Kathmandu; poet; essayist; playwright; linguist; columnist; translator; critic; author of multiple books*

Dr. Joshi does not prefer to conceptualize that the game rule of spiritualism is incompatible with the game rule of science. Where the vision of science ends, and where the revelation of spiritual mind begins are not diverse quests. The complementarity is expressed in his poems. I enjoy reading Dr. Joshi's profound expressions. A man of science with aesthetic zeal is the poet to read.

– *Arun Gupto, PhD, professor of English, IACER, Pokhara University, Kathmandu; author*

Dr. Mohan Joshi's *A Hundred Flowers to Awareness and Death* are pure songs of the soul as whispered effortlessly during day-to-day living. They are short and simple, yet profound in the messages they transmit and the lingering impact they leave. Each poem lifts the spirit and ends by transporting the reader to a place of peace and joy. In many ways, Dr. Joshi talks of the need to dwell in awareness.

– *Professor Tulasi Diwasa, folklore expert; poet; author of multiple books on culture, folklore, and poetry*

The poems in Mohan Prasad Joshi's *A Hundred Flowers to Awareness and Death* eloquently capture the cosmic connection between life and death, reflecting the poet's profound yearning for knowledge as a means to live life to its fullest. As a member of the Nepali diaspora in the US, Joshi speaks through these poems to the universality of human experiences, while simultaneously drawing on the distinct perspectives and cultural traditions of his homeland.

– Khem K. Aryal, PhD, associate professor, Department of English, Arkansas State University; author; literary editor

Mohan Joshi's *A Hundred Flowers to Awareness and Death* is like William Wordsworth's The Prelude. It is the poet's spiritual document where he describes awareness and death as two sides of the same coin. The mystery of awareness, so near, yet so far, so real, yet so surreal, baffles him and leads him to ask, "can you show me for once what exactly you look like?" It is the poet's conviction that both life and death can co-create synergistically an awareness that transcends them both. Awareness is the dominant motif that lends to Joshi's anthology logical coherence, unity of purpose, and consistency in thematic treatment.

– Mohan P Lohani, PhD, former professor and head, Central Department of English, Tribhuvan University, Kathmandu; former Nepalese ambassador to Bangladesh

Filled with references to the natural world and replete with vivid imagery and metaphors, this is a profound literary creation that delves deep into the human psyche. Prof. Joshi's moving and powerful poems evoke deep emotions and contemplation. Another standout feature in the anthology is the author's use of death as a theme. Rather than fearing death, Joshi uses it as an occasion to reflect on the fleeting nature of life and the importance of living in the present moment. I can see the book changing the mind of many people on how we look at life and death.

– Basant Pant, MD, PhD, neurosurgeon

MY FEW WORDS

Who sees all that is seen? Who breathes? Who talks and who becomes silent? Am I my name? Am I what society made me? Am I my identity? Do I cease to exist when my name and identity are gone? Who remains even when they no longer are? That's the place where I want to be. That's where life and death happen and all other things happen in their original, pristine form. That sweet spot has been my beloved. Getting it, losing it, and getting it again and losing it again for decades and decades—that's the bittersweet story. My short poems sing that story.

I keep wondering why I repeatedly attain and then lose that sweet spot? Why am I not there all the time? Decades and decades have passed, and this finding-losing game continues. Does losing it allow me to rejoice in its subsequent regainment? That beloved sweet spot is like the glasses I wear; I repeatedly lose them because of distractions and forgetfulness and the junk that constantly accumulates in and around me. And, when I feel handicapped and distressed without my glasses, I search. Then I find them and see clearly, myself and the world. My beloved glasses help me see things as they are, in their right size, at the right distance, without distortion, without blurring. What a sight that is!

I have discovered two tools that help me weed out the recurring junk of name and identity—awareness and death. I've observed that the tool of death sharpens the tool of awareness. Like rain settles the contaminants suspended in the air, I find that a periodic shower of remembering our impermanence washes away the pollutants dirtying our mind and gives uninterrupted access to pure awareness, in which everything is.

The hundred poems in this collection are hymns to those two tools—the tool of remembering our mortal nature and the tool of watching the nature of our awareness. The tools work in complementary and synergistic ways to shift me back to a peaceful and blissful dimension of living from a place of chaos and suffering. The poems are a way of expressing my gratitude, saying my 'thank you' to them.

I wish to express my gratitude to those who helped me in various ways as I worked on this anthology. Martha Embrey and Professor Padma Prasad Devkota read the final drafts of my manuscript and suggested some word edits, most of which I accepted. I am thankful to Professor Govinda Raj Bhattarai, Professor Abhi Subedi, Professor Deepak Shimkhada, Professor D.C. Chambial, Rosemerry Wahtola Trommer, Nabin K Chhetri, Professor Shreedhar Lohani, Professor Sanjeev Uprety, Professor Mohan P. Lohani, Professor Arun Gupto, Professor Tulasi Diwasa, Dr. Basant Pant, and Khem Aryal for their endorsements. My wife Rajani Joshi and daughter Aditi Joshi lovingly read or listened to my poems and motivated me to write more. I had my 93-year-old mother Neeleshwari Devi Joshi's blessing and my late father Professor Dr. Tara Prasad Joshi's loving memory when each poem arose in me. And our sweet family member, Everest, who lives with us in the form of a little dog, was silent but powerful company as the poems came to me. A lot of learning happened living with Everest.

Mohan Prasad Joshi, MD, MSc, MBBS

Sterling, Virginia, USA

January 2025

CONTENTS

THE PAGE NUMBERS LISTED IN THIS TABLE OF CONTENTS APPLY ONLY TO THE PRINT VERSION OF THE BOOK, NOT TO THE E-BOOK VERSION.

Praise for A Hundred Flowers to Awareness and Death – vii

My few words – xiii

Bird on the camphor tree – 1
Everest gave me a lesson – 3
The art of dying – 5
Fresh and new – 6
What made my eyes collide with you? – 8
Make me a new phoenix every moment – 9
A period at the end of a well-made sentence – 10
Perhaps the trio wants to go deeper – 11
Lend me your hearts and souls – 13
Gateway to my destination – 14
This and next rock 'n' roll – 16
Rise – 17
An experiment I used to enjoy – 18
Narrative change needed – 19
What the river told me – 20
Game changer – 21
Where's the now? – 22

Suffering! – 23
The bridge – 24
Operate life from that place – 26
Expound a new definition – 27
Middle of the night – 28
A letter from death – 29
Everest – 30
Someday, somewhere – 31
Pigeons on the parapet – 32
Everything's going to be alright – 33
Like when my thoughts stopped – 34
The song I heard this morning – 36
Wink at each other – 37
A day off from active management – 38
Big mirror – 39
Hachiko – a dog to remember – 40
No more grand wishes – 41
Breaking Free – 42
Lost my reference point – 43
Why wait? – 44
I live on – 45
Won't waste time looking at a rainbow – 46
Gangrene of me and thee – 48
A river's journey – 49
Colocasia leaf – 50
Life – you look good! – 51
Always lived – 52
Serendipitous research finding – 53
What I found with my investigation – 55
Dear Dad! – 57
Cast his piercing eyes on me – 59
Seeing a bird – 60
Time to ask me – 61

Circle – 62
Always missed the gaps – 63
Chant poems – 64
Millions of possibilities – 65
Motherly lap – 66
Without a glass wall in between – 68
The shapes of the clouds – 69
I'm aware that I'm watching – 70
Without a sigh – 71
Languages can't encompass me – 72
Earth – 73
Antivirus – 75
False character – 76
Forgive me – 77
Died instantly – 78
The world was born – 79
Won't hesitate to bid a final adieu – 80
For you – 81
I'll rise above you – 82
The only barrier between me and liberation – 83
Perfect as is – 84
Death, you're not what they say – 85
Unpredictable joker – 86
Blended therapy – 87
Traveling light – 88
With no tie around my neck – 89
Lost and found – 90
It continues – 91
Great Olympic moment – 92
The same dough dwells in them – 93
All there is, is seeing – 94
Beautiful at the borderline – 95
Filling every alveolus of my lungs – 96

Just that, nothing more – 98
Rising in spirals – 99
Can't wait to reach home and sit again – 100
Looking up in freedom with hands outstretched – 101
I glimpsed You – 102
Sorry for what I've done to you – 103
What has life done? – 105
A sharp arrow – 106
I'm stuck where I am – 107
Seriously! Are you dumb? – 108
Whose is all this? – 109
Dear life! – 110
Can you show me for once? – 111
Last night was strange – 112
Miles and miles – 113
You're my two sides – 114
One flower to awareness and one to death – 115

About the author – 117

~ ~

POEMS

Bird on the camphor tree

Hey birdie! I heard your chirping.
It's only 3:30 in the morning.
But it's ok – I have been sleeping for a long time.
Better that I wake up.

I heard your simple, sweet, and soothing voice.
I heard your sound, your music,
without words, concepts, or images.

I thanked the vibrations
that travelled from your syrinx
to the labyrinths of my ears
and celebrated the lucky chance
that my window was open in between them.

And as I was writing these lines,
you suddenly stopped chirping.
That gave me an epiphany
as to how your voice
and the silence of the space
were taking turns

exposing and amplifying
each other's beauty.

Birdie, you seem to like
the camphor tree in my garden.
I hope you will continue to come
and sit on it and chirp from there
during our future mornings.
I'll ensure my window remains open
so that I can hear you well
when you call.

Everest gave me a lesson

Our little dog, Everest, looked at me,
sensing my unhappiness.
He raised his right front paw
and gently hit my chest.

Having lived with him for seven years,
I now know his looks and actions.
I'm pretty sure his eyes were saying –
    Why are you unhappy, grandpa?
    Look at me. I'm happy with what I have—
    I have my life, I have the day to live it,
    and I have you who takes care of me.
    You have everything I have and much more,
    yet you seem to ignore it all
    and focus on what you don't have.
    Get out of this habit, grandpa,
    and just be happy, like me.
    I'm with you, you're with me, and life is with us.
    Let's enjoy it together, at this moment,
    without piling any other conditions.

In silence I took him on my lap
and gently scratched him behind his ears—
behind my Everest's happy ears.

The art of dying

The autumn leaves play
a festival of colors as they die,
decorating trees
and the ground underneath
with orange, red, brown, and yellow.

They die giving joy to passersby,
job to photographers,
nourishment to the roots,
and space for new leaves
to come out in the spring.

What a way to end
the journey, like an old lady,
her face fully made up,
slipping into the unknown
with a smile on her face!

Fresh and new

I'm through with the long-wasted years
of planning and calculating.
I'm now changing the way I live
and want to live one day at a time.
Every day I want to be new and fresh for that day.

What I kept remembering from the past didn't help
and what I kept planning didn't happen.
All that happened was something else.
So why waste time in a futile indulgence!
Instead, I want to use the time I have
to live today, for real.

I want to do what each moment calls for,
as I just did – I parked my car
at the Thornton Overlook on the Shenandoah Skyline Drive
and looked down and across at the many layers
of tapering hills rising from a tiny valley in the center.

And I glanced at the Overlook's visitor information board.
Its title read, *The Many Moods of the Overlook.*
Underneath the title were several pictures
of the valley from different seasons,
and at the bottom was the age-old haunting quote

from the Greek philosopher Heraclitus of Ephesus –
   No man ever steps into the same river twice,
      for it's not the same river and he's not the same man.

What made my eyes collide with you?

Oh, winter trees!
Who made my eyes collide
with you today and witness
your branches swaying in the wind?
Did you say –
    I'm bare and still dancing!

Oh, fallen, lone, dried, and curled-up leaf!
I see you effortlessly rolling
from right to left on the road,
softly propelled by the wind,
as if to tell me to slow down my car
and give a good look at you.

Oh, fallen trees!
I see you're slowly rotting
on the ground to feed the roots
of those alive and standing.
What made my eyes collide with you today
and why?

Make me a new phoenix every moment

Death—I worship you, invoke you.
Come close and teach me
the secrets of living well.

People shun you; I call upon you.
I sing to you. Come and live with me
and give me a life worth living.

Keep burning and turning
all my accumulated memories
into ashes from which I can rise

as a new phoenix every moment, ever fresh,
unlike the mythical one that must wait
500 years to rise again as a new bird.

A period at the end of a well-made sentence

I left something unfinished
and wandered around
for long – so long
I can't even remember.

I had forgotten totally,
but strange, unbelievable circumstances
worked together to take me back
to that unfinished task.

I recall doing nothing on my own
in the entire process. Then who was it
that pulled and propelled
the wandering and aimless me back to that task?!

Whoever or whatever it was,
when the task was finished,
it felt like contentedly putting a period
at the end of a well-written sentence.

Perhaps the trio wants to go deeper

Deep in the night,
my eyes are open,
feeling the silence
and watching the darkness
that reveal secrets.

The inner side of my left arm
presses against the temple of my head
and feels the pulsing
of the superficial temporal artery.

The fingers of my right hand
slide under the drawstring of my pajamas
and feel my abdomen
rise and fall
with each breath.

I hear the AC unit turn on
to cool the July air,
and my skin and lungs
feel that coolness.

Then I hear thunder
far up in the sky,

that hops out in pulses
and fades into silence.

Scared by the sound,
our little dog, Everest, runs to me
and curls up against my waist.
I make a cup with my right hand
and hold his tiny back paws
to reassure him that he's safe.

I take an easy, deep breath
and salute the trio
of darkness, silence, and awareness.

My eyes slowly begin to close.
Perhaps the trio wants to go deeper.

Lend me your hearts and souls

Poets of the past
from all over the world!
Lend me your hearts,
lend me your souls

so that I can witness the beauty
bare winter trees carry,
and see agony, emptiness, and death
as my gurus

and use those new learnings
to shift from an ignorant
to an aware life
filled with bliss

of writing and reading poems,
as you would,
on the trinity
of *suffering, search, and solution.*

Gateway to my destination

Why go to a shrine out there
on a mountain or an island, or in a jungle
when you're my shrine!
You're the visible half,
and I pray to you to connect me
with the invisible half reigning inside.

You're not just my body. You're a gateway
to my destination! A friend you are,
communicating silently all the time.
Through you my soul sings, awareness shines.
The bliss of existence is through you,
not by denying or damning you.

All your cells are intelligent,
working individually and together
to make a unified me. It's a wonder
how you breathe for me,
speak for me, and artfully hold a cup
with your fingers and drink from it.

Distracted and indulged, I exhausted you
for decades and ignored your silent signals.
But now I try to keep you calm

like an unrippled lake,
and wait for my inner half to show up
and swim in your still waters.

This and next rock 'n' roll

Awareness,
you've only been an occasional guest.
Please be a constant companion
and help fulfill my two goals:

Goal 1
Dance with life,
chant for life, 24/7,
all the way to the end.

Goal 2
At the transit point,
send off a few goodbye rhythms
to the old
and step, with a smiley face,
into the new
to start the next phase of rock 'n' roll.

Rise

Rise
in me and defeat
the billion-knotted bundle
called my mind.

Thoughts, its brutal soldiers,
splatter blood all the time
on the screen
of my consciousness.

Tackling individual thoughts hasn't helped –
even before I pierce one, the next one pops up,
outpacing my abilities to win the battle. So, come
to my rescue and attack the factory, attack my mind,

by unveiling yourself and showing your face!
Give an audience and stun my mind! Let it surrender,
with all its arms and armies, at your feet and get liberated,
by seeing that you are the source and NOT it.

Awareness! Rise
in me and defeat
the billion-knotted bundle
called my mind.

An experiment I used to enjoy

A simple experiment I used to enjoy:

At the cinema, my eyes would be seeing the movie,
and my awareness would see me and others
watching the movie, witnessing real-time
how one gets identified and engaged

with the screen characters
and drowns in emotions.
Every time I had this inclusive sight from a distance,
I would no longer be under the movie's spell.

It used to be revealing,
like a CCTV, mounted high up on a pole,
quietly capturing all the traffic and commotion
on the street down below.

Narrative change needed

More than a 100 of the 108 billion people
that have ever lived, are no more.
Where are they now?
Back to the water, air, fire, earth
and space they came from.

Arising from them,
returning to them,
and in between, living in them,
yet we see them as mere physical elements,
just to be used and exploited.

Isn't it time we *revived the art*
of treating them with deference,
as the ancients did,
instead of raving nonstop
that we've conquered them?

What the river told me

I often go to a river I like.
When I was there this morning, I asked a question –
    Dear River, tell me, am I the same person
    who used to visit you 30 years back?

Before the river could answer, I heard myself shout out loud –
    But of course, you're the same,
    with just a few wrinkles on your face, some grey hairs,
    and a pair of glasses over your eyes.

When silence returned, the River whispered –
    Your outside may seem the same,
    but much has flown through your inside,
    availing of you as a vehicle,

    just as my banks and bed look pretty much as they were
    30 years back, but much water has flown ever since,
    and every time you visited me,
    the water you saw was new and fresh.

Game changer

In an evening in the year 2000,
at the foothills of a mountain near Kathmandu,
I was walking, watching a collaborative performance

of the clouds and sunrays on the screen of the sky,
when a bigger performance suddenly flashed,
subsuming all that I was seeing.

Dazed, I stood still in that alive oneness.
Minutes passed before I and my mind returned.
Only then returned the separateness of other objects.

Well, that was all it was, but was a game changer.
When I was walking back home that evening,
I already had a seed planted in me.

Now in 2023, after twenty-three years,
I see that tiny seed grown into a large tree
under whose shade I often sit in Virginia.

Where's the now?

Between the dead *past*
and the *future* that's not there,
where's the *now*?

With all the three absent,
what's left
to achieve or renounce?

These burdens out of my way,
I see freedom
walking into me.

Suffering!

Dear suffering –
you've been a true guru.

Great learnings happened
when you were total,

giving my mind—a perpetual complainer—
no way out.

The bridge

March 19, 2023. Quiet Sunday morning.
Chilly with temperature of 26°F at 8am.
Just came back from a short walk
with Everest, our sweet little dog

and as I was taking off his boots and harness,
I heard the usual doom and gloom on the TV –
    The economy is going down
      and we're likely to go into a bigger war.

I needed a second walk and headed out.
I was well-dressed for the cold morning
and had on a muffler, gaiter, and cap,
besides my warm jacket and gloves.

I glanced up and saw a bird floating in the sky,
with its body shining in the yellow sun rays.
Happy it looked, gliding against the vastness
and listening to the cosmic silence.

I was on the ground and the bird was up there,
but an unseen bridge suddenly connected us
and I began receiving the bird's energy.
I forgot the TV's doom and gloom

and felt as free and happy as the bird.
Within moments, I was flying with it
against the unending blue of the sky,
listening to the cosmic silence.

Operate life from that place

One day
I felt like dying to everything
that could die.

Boldly, I started dying
to the myriads of what I was
and what I knew.

After everything mortal died,
I got stuck at a place where I couldn't die
to *that* in whom the game of dying was playing.

Then I wondered –
where's death
if I learn to operate life from that place!

Expound a new definition

Alive! Alive! Look here! Look there,
look everywhere – everything's alive!

Find a thing that's not alive?
Jump out of the box to redefine

what aliveness is. Go beyond
saying alive is one that's not dead.

Time to be bold and see
that everything's alive and in action,

adapting, growing, shrinking, and evolving.
Speak to the valley – it echoes back.

Jump into the river; it takes you to the ocean.
Get into the ocean and ride along the waves.

Eat a mango and swallow its sweetness.
Just look around to see how alive

everything is, developing, dancing,
disappearing and reappearing.

Middle of the night

In the middle of the night,
I woke up to a thoughtless awareness
of a faint snoring of Everest,

our darling Cavapoo, sleeping with his tiny paws
over the vertex of my head,
as if to transmit peace to me

and I woke up to a little ache in my right neck
that I've been having for many years.
All was good in the witnessing of that suchness.

A letter from death

Recently, D sent me a letter,
short and sweet, saying –
> Don't die before your death.
> Live fully while alive.
> Look at me and do so.
>
> Look at me at least once a day.
> A few times is even better.
> Contrary to what you've been told,
> you won't be depressed seeing me.
>
> Look at me to get inspired
> to give and to forgive
> and to finish today
> what you've left for tomorrow.

Everest

Our little dog Everest
lives up to his name. He makes his life easy
as if he were simply watching it
from the summit of Everest.

His abdominal breathing with body relaxed on the floor.
Effortless attention to every sound, sight, and movement, near and far.
The trust he displays through his belly-up sleep with paws in the air.
Bursts of exuberant playing followed by his superman positions.
His wriggling movements and wagging tail when we're back home.
His steady, long, unblinking, and penetrating look at us
when he is hungry or needs to attend to his nature calls.
The therapeutic joy he brings through his mere presence.

•

There's a lot to learn from his life
lived in ebullience and relaxation, combined perfectly.
A lot to learn from how he attains and distributes happiness
through his trust and surrender
and a simple presence to the present moment.

Someday, somewhere

A little teardrop rolled down
the corner of my left eye
to the side of my nose and woke me up.

My finger felt and wiped the teardrop,
bringing the *memory of an ancient time*
when we were together.

And here I'm sleeping sideways,
silently crying, not knowing
when we'll meet again.

It's been very long. But I know,
someday, somewhere,
I'll feel your fingers wiping my tears.

Pigeons on the parapet

Last night, I woke up with the sounds of a pelting rain and colliding clouds
and I wondered who woke up hearing those sounds?

I must have returned to sleep, as I had an awareness of waking up again this morning.
And I pondered – who returned to sleep and who woke up, refreshed?

The morning was cold. I donned a sweatshirt and looked out the window.
A few pigeons were sitting on the parapet of my neighbor's terrace.

They were all facing the East, quiet and motionless. And again, I wondered –
who witnessed those pigeons saluting the sun in silence?

And I felt – that's who I am.

Everything's going to be alright

The dull ache permeating all my being,
the uneasy awareness of my heart thumping,
legs lying heavy with a wooden feeling,
eyes and ears no longer wanting to see and hear,
and a wish for my breath to quietly cease
at the end of a long exhalation.

Still, amid all these feelings,
I don't know how and why
an untouched part in me sits serenely
with the assurance
that everything's going to be alright!

Like when my thoughts stopped

Like when my thoughts stopped
as the ground underneath me
suddenly rocked left and right
from a big earthquake in Kathmandu,

like when a giant roller-coaster
I rode in Sweden plunged down
with super speed, giving me
a feeling of an approaching end,

like how the world around me ceased
when I saw my father's lifeless body
whose feet were living when I had bowed
to them only a couple of hours back,

like what I saw blew away my mind
when I dared to peep at the midday Sun
through a little crevice
between my interlaced fingers,

and like when a big bang woke me up
from sleeping at the wheels
to witness the smoke and inflated airbags in my car
crushed at the Capital Beltway,

let my mind always live with an acute awareness
of the reality as is, at the immediacy of the moment,
without the disrupting thoughts
of the dead past and imaginary future.

The song I heard this morning

My old age plan to enjoy relaxed days
with my retirement savings,
my wish to leave behind a name on this earth
that people may remember long after I'm gone,
and one thousand other desires brewing in me,
including the one to understand
who I am before I die.

What'll happen to all these plans
should something else happen?
That has been my constant fear.

But a song I overheard this morning
suddenly emboldened me
to look straight at the face of Fear
and say –
      Go away! Need you no more,
      as I need to live right now.

Qué será, será
What will be, will be.

Wink at each other

Sometime back, Death and I
came face to face and we smiled.

Strangely, I opened the inner pocket
of my jacket and D slipped into it.

Since then, my walk on the street of life
has been easy-peasy and painless.

The ads, the crowds, the cacophony
no longer distract or bother me.

Occasionally, however, they still do
due to the remnants of my old habits.

When that happens, I pull out D
from my pocket for a second.

We wink at each other and my walk
on the street of life eases again.

A day off from active management

After half a century of active management,
I decided to experiment on letting life live
on its own for one day.

No concepts, no policies, no frameworks, no designs,
nor any strategies, guidelines, or plans
to direct its actions that day.

Also, life got time off from who I was, where I lived,
what I did, what I liked and what I didn't.
And at the end of the day, when I checked back

on my life, I was pleasantly surprised
to see that it hadn't fallen off any cliffs,
and that its intact face was beaming with gratitude!

Big mirror

I want to stand naked,
completely naked,
in front of a big mirror that can reflect
the whole of me as I am.

I want to see and face everything
that I've been hiding for decades.
Let me look at myself
as others would look at me,

identifying every color I've painted
and every tumor I've allowed to grow in my body,
every smell I've allowed to putrefy in my orifices,
and every hurtful word I've flung out of my mouth.

I want to identify the impact they have had
to disfigure this beautiful gift.
Yes, I want to examine how every part,
every organ of my body I've damaged.

Consciousness! I've heard you're the best clinician.
Please stand in front of me as a big dustless mirror.
I promise, I'll do my best to partner with you
to bring about my own healing.

Hachiko – a dog to remember

Hachiko!
It's been nearly 100 years
and your spirit lives on
guiding humans in millions
on what devotion is, friendship is.

You waited for ten long years
at the Shibuya train station for your master
from the day he didn't return
to greet you back at the station
as he'd died that day at work.

As I sit and watch the tears
of gratitude still welling
in your master Ueno's spirit eyes,
my own tears and forehead drop
on your spirit feet.

No more grand wishes

No more wishes
for a great future, remarkable life.

All I want is an easy breath
at this moment

in a healthy body with a mirror-like mind,
reflecting the universe as is.

Breaking free

I finally rejected
the decades-long helplessness and subjugation
to the self-proclaimed master, my mind,
and revolted out to be a free body,
just as Celie broke herself free
from her abusive husband, Albert,
in the movie *Color Purple*.

And just as Celie finally found
her dear sister Nettie's letters to her,
cruelly hidden by Albert for many years,
I discovered how my trickster mind was hiding
the messages my soul had been sending
for decades. But now the two of us are together
without the trickster in-between.

Lost my reference point

With no five-letter identity as h-u-m-a-n,
I shifted from seeing the differences
to seeing similarities in all creatures.

With no reference point to work from,
I no longer needed to play the game of name
and worry about exhibiting my personality.

Freed from being a little piece of named art
confined to an isolated canvas, I became
part of a limitless art in the sky of awareness.

Why wait?

Why do I keep making plans to visit
famed places to see their grandeur?

Why can't I see the grandeur
of whatever's around me,

here and now,
just as the dew drops

on the needles of a pine tree
that I just passed by during my morning walk!

I live on

Bite me, eat me.
Hit me where it hurts most.
Tear apart what you can
and take away pieces of my physicality.

Yet, your might will not work,
and you'll be frustrated.
No tools from your workshop
can eliminate the deathless in me.

Destroy the house, but the space
on which it was built lives on.
Shoot the sky, but you can't create
holes in my empty integrity.

Seal my mouth, pierce my larynx,
but how will you silence
the unstruck note deep in me,
reverberating timelessly?

Won't waste time looking at a rainbow

A hard-working super-achiever,
I'm always active, ever busy,
finishing task after task
through excellence in multitasking
even at the dinner table
and the art of staying up all night!

I run after every single opportunity.
My time is my asset, and I don't waste it
resting and relaxing.
One life and so much to do,
calling for smart decisions
on what I do and what I don't.
For example, I won't waste time
looking at a rainbow,
when I know well that its beauty is nothing
but an illusion in the sky
appearing from a play of sunrays
with tiny raindrops—simple physics.

I know how to succeed and shine
by ceaselessly pushing myself beyond limits,
and managing every minute of my time—

how can I waste it
resting, relaxing, meditating
and foolishly staring at a rainbow!

Gangrene of me and thee

At rest
at last

after amputating
my I

gone blue
with the gangrene

of me
and thee.

A river's journey

A river is on a seemingly endless journey,
pulled and propelled by a mysterious magnet
beyond her grasp.

She runs restless and thirsty, not knowing
where she's heading, what she's searching,
but a day is soon coming

when she'll morph into the very ocean
she pours into, quenching her thirst
and ending her search.

Colocasia leaf

A colocasia leaf lets water
glide playfully down its surface
as beautiful beads
while never itself getting wet.

I wish I had the skin and spirit
of a colocasia leaf to play plentifully
with life with my clothes
always clean, always unrumpled.

Life – you look good!

An overnight-soaked assortment
of one thousand seeds of legumes—
chickpeas, Bengal grams, kidney beans
green moong, black-eyed peas,
black beans, and lima beans—
germinated in two days,

each seed letting life pop out
as a curious shoot
ready to expand, explore and experience.

Ah! The smell and sight of life!
The will to whoop and witness!

Always lived

With my head between the pillow
and the blanket covering it, and the body curled up
in a fetal position, my eyes watched the darkness inside
that slowly turned into my warm, dark days
in the womb of my mother.

From there on, I continued to regress,
first into my parents' seeds
that formed the fetus that I became,
and then into the seeds of my parents' parents, and
further on into the preceding parents' roots.

As I continued to recede, I realized –
as life, I've always lived.
Only my individual forms have come and gone.

Serendipitous research finding

Context

- Taking my dog to the backyard morning and evening for his nature calls.

Materials and methods

- Two containers lying in the open in the backyard, one empty and the other filled with weeds and waste.
- It rained suddenly, triggering an uninitiated experiment.

Results noticed serendipitously

- The empty container got filled with pure rainwater.
- The other trapped very little water and that too got contaminated.
- A crow landed on the first container and drank the clean water from it, looked around with satisfied eyes, and flew away.

Conclusion

- An already full container can't fill fresh water that a crow enjoys.

What I found with my investigation

This morning my doorbell rang.
I saw a package delivered on the porch
and a FedEx employee walk away.

As I was opening the contents of the package,
I liked the bubble-wrapped envelope,
with my name printed on it,
and put it on my bookshelf for future use.

Right then, I noticed something
that made me look back at the shelf. OMG!
It had loads of similar package wraps I had placed in the past.
Curious, I looked at the study table – same there,
with a third of it covered with all kinds of junk.

That prompted me to investigate a bit further –
I went up to my bedroom and opened the chest of drawers.
Phew! Again junk, more junk—
wraps of tools and gadgets ordered from Amazon,
old pens that no longer write,
stacks of utility bills from decades back,
and bottles of long-expired medicines,
all covered with a thin layer of fine dust.

Half-amused, half-annoyed, I went down to the basement
to continue the investigation, where I needed to walk carefully
between the shoes, furniture, clothes, and containers
that I hadn't used for years nor was I ever likely to.

Walking back up, I saw the living room no different either—
old magazines and junk mail on the center table
that also had three empty coffee mugs and two teacups,
a half-filled bag of chips lying open, an empty coke can,
and half a dozen remotes with four from my old TVs.

The kitchen surprised me even more
as the rear halves of the countertops, cabinets, and the fridge
had stuff I became aware of
only because I looked at them intentionally.

Naturally, I got a bit tired and sat on the sofa
in the family room next to the kitchen,
pressed my interlocked fingers and palms
behind my skull and looked up at the ceiling
and admired the spiderwebs,
some of which were extending from the chandelier
to the crown molding. My eyes closed.

Behind the closed eyelids appeared
the multi-storied, multi-roomed house of my life.
The situation there wasn't any different either.
All the rooms were cluttered
and the most cluttered of all was the one called my mind!

Dear Dad!

Dear Dad!
I had heard the questions you'd asked
sitting on the terrace
during the second half of your life –
    Where will I be going?
    What will I be doing?

Today, when I saw your picture
in the prayer room,
I remembered
those questions of yours.

Wherever you are,
I hope you're okay, you're well.
If possible, come into my dream and tell me
what you've been doing
in all these 37 years
since you went away.
I'm impatient to know about you,
to hear from you.

Although invisible outside,
the undercurrent of your memory
is constantly running
inside the river of my life.

The memories of the moments
I spent with you during my childhood
continue to live as unwithered flowers
in the temple of my mind.

While coming to my dream,
please hint at some answers
to those same questions
that are now appearing to me too –
    Where will I be going?
    What will I be doing?

Cast his piercing eyes on me

I was looking at a hawk
flying with ease
in the sky.

The hawk suddenly swooped,
and coming close,
cast his piercing eyes on me

and said in silence –
    Go
    with the wind's flow.

    Flap less and glide more,
    like a hawk,
    with effortless elegance in the sky.

Seeing a bird

The sight of a bird
on a tree branch

evoked a question in me:

did a separate *seer see* the *seen*,
or was it three-in-one?

Time to ask me

Driving for decades
at a fast speed,

my joints ache, and
my mind shakes.

Time to ask me –
should I

continue to run, run, run
or relax a bit and have some fun

by changing my role
from a driver to a passenger?

Circle

In the figure below,

○

the dot in the center suddenly spoke –
    Circling for ages!
    If you feel you've reached nowhere,
    try making a small change!
    Simply step out of your circle
    and start walking inwards.
    That's all it takes.

Always missed the gaps

The gazillion stars dazzled me
while I always missed the gaps between them,

the same way I always missed the silence between the sounds
and the gaps between my thoughts.

I voraciously read millions of lines in hundreds of books,
but always missed reading the space between the lines,

and here I'm drowning in the ocean of knowledge
with no wisdom to stay afloat.

Chant poems

Alone, I walk,
fearless and confident
but alert,
like a tiger,
in the vagarious jungle
of life,

and often I groom,
like a cat,
to clean the dirt,
release the mats,
and cool off the heat
that this jungle generates,

and above all, like a bird,
I continuously chant poems,
pure and pacific,
to ward off evil thoughts
of jealousy, hatred, arrogance
and the like,

so that I can stay sane
in this insane jungle.

Millions of possibilities

As pollens willing
to be dispersed
create future flowers
at distant places,

give me the
burst of courage
to blow away
into millions of possibilities!

Motherly lap

I bow to you,
Darkness!

You're the base
on which little dots of stars
appear,

you're the silence
against which the faint sounds
of colliding galaxies are heard,

and you're the ultimate
into which space, time,
everything and all finally return.

Personally, what I like most about you
is that at the end of each day,
you come to me as night,

close my eyes,
and give me the bliss of sleep
on your motherly lap,

so, I can wake up the next morning,
recharged and ready
to deal with the day.

Without a glass wall in between

The quarter-century-old oaks
standing tall in my backyard
greeted me vibrantly,
as I opened the sliding door to our deck.
And suddenly, I realized it'd been months
since I last looked at our backyard.

Right then, running down
came our little dog, Everest,
who seized that opportunity to see and feel
the raindrops falling on our deck,
without the barrier of a glass wall
standing in between.

With his canine nose, repeatedly
he sniffed the open world,
especially the air
infused with the smell of the wet earth,
and looked up at the trees and the sky,
in wonder!

The shapes of the clouds

How powerful the clouds
of yesteryears were,
making shapes everywhere!

Sometimes they used to march
as massive elephants
and sometimes as angry giants.

Even today, the clouds in the sky
and thought-clouds in my mind
continue to come and roam in large numbers

but, powerlessly, they fizzle out after a while,
as dead and gone is my old habit
of projecting shapes on them.

I'm aware that I'm watching

Spring has come.
I'm sitting in my room.
Gnats are flying outside the window.
A dog is barking at a distance.
Two little trees are swaying in the wind
and their tender leaves look yellow
against the light of the setting sun.

The sky looks blue and empty
except for a small patch of clouds.
A few birds enter my field of vision,
fly towards the West and disappear.
The sky becomes empty again.
The little patch of clouds also disappears.

I'm sitting and watching all this.
I'm also aware that I'm watching.
There's no desire, no ripple,
with everything in place,
everything as is,
in this pure awareness.

Without a sigh

May I always remember
today could be my last day
and tonight, my last night.
If I wake up tomorrow,
may I remember to say,
"I got another day."

May each day
be filled with
the goodness of an entire life,
so that if I lived 100 years,
it'd be like 100 lives
lived well in one life.

And on my last day,
may I have
the quality of a ripe fruit
ready to detach
from the tree
without a wound or a sigh.

Languages can't encompass me

You don't see me
but I'm present,
like salt in water
and fragrance in the air.

Drink like a fish,
and you'll get the taste.
Sniff like a dog,
and you'll get the smell.

Languages don't encompass,
definitions don't capture,
words don't contain,
and thoughts don't grasp me.

I appear as awareness
when they all disappear,
just as the Sun appears
as soon as the clouds disappear.

Earth

I had a dream of an interplanetary voyage in our solar system.

Journey to the other planets -
Mercury made me flee right away as it had no atmosphere, besides being too hot on one side and too cold on the other.
Venus wasn't suitable either, with all its heat and dense clouds.
Mars was very cold, and so were the gas giants, *Jupiter, Saturn,* and *Uranus.*
I barely survived being sucked into the titanic storms raging on Jupiter.
The deceptively beautiful *Saturn* was inhospitable with all its hydrogen gas.
Neptune, the ice giant, and *Pluto,* the dwarf planet, were terribly cold.

Return journey to home -
As I approached closer to the *Earth,* I started getting excited but was soon taken aback when I saw tears in her eyes.
She was so sweet and kind to offer me her lap as soon as I landed
and give me her water and food. And to my surprise, she spoke, "Child! You must be tired. Have some rest and we'll talk later."
I slept right away.

•

I woke up, refreshed,
and the two of us started to talk.
Sensing I was in a relaxed mood (and not angry as I usually am),
she opened up about her sorrows and feelings:
"Child! I'm suffering with all that's going on—my health is down and soul sad.
I have a rising temperature and my polluted lungs can't breathe.
My beautiful clothes—my forests—are disappearing, making me naked.
My arteries and veins are filled with sewage.
My ice caps are melting, exposing my head, and submerging my body.
My other children—your siblings—are displaced and dying in massive numbers.
Can you please help!"

•

The dream ended there. I woke up with a feeling of sadness,
looked at the ceiling of my room for a few minutes,
and went to the window and opened the blinds.
The morning light flooded my room.

I looked at the tree standing in my front yard. A robin was sitting on it.
And I suddenly realized that the tree, the robin, and I were all lit
with the same awareness.
For the first time, I felt very close to the tree and the robin.
For the first time, I saw them as my siblings.

Antivirus

You delete the cookies, tags, and cache
stored in the mind from its play
with a gazillion data floating in the universe.

How infected and destructive life would be
without the antivirus effect you have
on our megalomaniac egos' treacherous malwares.

Dear death, may I remember to let you scan
the laptop of my life on a regular basis
so that it remains safe and optimally functional.

False character

I searched my mind long
for a solution, for an answer.
I failed.
Now I realize, I was asking
a character of a dream
to help me.

The character gave me much—
twists, turns, and tantrums,
and a lot of pleasure,
pain, and palpitation
from its convoluted actions
in the dream story.

Then, one day, when I woke up,
the dream disappeared
and it became clear
that I was asleep, dreaming,
relying on a character
that was itself false.

Forgive me

Forgive me, Sun, forgive me, Moon.
Forgive me, birds and trees,
and rains and rivers.
I ignored you and choreographed my life

without drawing inspirations from you.
I infused loads of myself,
and none of your energies
in directing my life.

And here's my life's movie playing,
packed with acts of agitation,
with no calming scenes
of rest and peace!

Died instantly

I was pacing about my room
with a hundred worries in my head
and nausea in my stomach.
All looked gloomy and dark.
My body shuddered, and my legs reeled.

Unable to stand any longer,
I sank into my sofa and looked out.
All I saw were those hundred worries
floating in front of my eyes.
Right then, something simple happened

that brought a profound shift in no time.
As I was breathing a heavy sigh,
my body and head lowered,
aligning my eyes
with the incoming sun rays.

As those late afternoon rays hit my retina,
my thoughts and worries died instantly.
All that was left was awareness shining,
just like the red Sun
glowing above the horizon.

The world was born

The cawing
of a
crow

was heard
in the depth
of space,

perceived
in the awareness,
arising in silence.

The world
was
born.

Won't hesitate to bid a final adieu

Is my friend a cheat? It seems so.
I've been collaborating with him

for 40 years to set me free
from the prison I think I'm in.

Lately, however, I've begun to doubt
his integrity. Why?

Because, when he sleeps at night,
the prison's four walls disappear,

only to reappear instantly
as he wakes up in the morning.

Investigation required! I'll spy
real-time now on my so-called best friend

and if caught red-handed, won't hesitate to say
then and there, "Bye-bye, dear cheating mind."

For you

My mind's moving,
pen too,
making a poem on you.

Eyes open,
heart too,
for a glimpse of you.

My body bows,
head too,
singing praises of you.

Speechless,
talking too,
contemplating on you.

Awareness!
Be with me
in life and death too.

I'll rise above you

You don't bring me a creation.
Look how productive the pains are
of a mother expecting soon,
a scientist nearing a discovery,
and an artist about to draw a masterpiece.

Sterile and futile pain – Yes, you are.
You're always there, like the womb
of a barren woman, making her cry in silence.
Always total, all-consuming, like a California fire,
mercilessly burning and spreading.

My body and brain are aching
but can you touch my awareness?
Abiding in it, I'm watching you,
and will keep watching, until I rise above you,
and bloom like a lotus, above the mud.

Don't think you'll prevail forever.

The only barrier between me and liberation

A gust of wind hit
my face hard and blew away

the million maggots of thoughts
feeding on the dead past

piled in my being. With that,
I instantly stepped into a world

of liberation, and laughed
upon seeing that the only barrier

between me and liberation
were my million thoughts!

Perfect as is

Each breath's an eternity.
Each look and each sound are the same,
with no wish to control anything.
Just relaxing in the knowingness—
all welcome with no exclusion.

How liberating this seeing is,
this seeing without any need to say
it's right or wrong,
this seeing without the me
filtering the incoming information.

With a shift from "I see" to "just seeing,"
a liberation happened.
All the burdens fell away,
all tasks finished.
Everything fell in place, everything was perfect.

Death, you're not what they say

Just your mention
makes them uncomfortable.
Any conversation about you
is a taboo.

They never befriend you
while alive and active.
So, when they must face you in the end,
they're unprepared.

They avoid you, constantly,
and miss out on living a life
filled with awareness,
which only you can catalyze.

They see you as a destroyer,
not knowing you're only like a fire
removing impurities from gold,
and letting it shine, pristine.

Unpredictable joker

So much I planned with you.
In the end you were the one who decided
what was to happen.

I tried to shape you, but you shattered
all my schemes and projects
and brought many erratic twists and turns.

Life, you're an unpredictable joker!
From now on, I'll no longer crave
a secure relationship with you.

I choose freedom from you.
You'll just be a street performer –
I'll watch your shows but no longer react.

You'll just be a cloud passing by.
My eyes will see you, but they'll be set
beyond you, into the deep blue sky.

Blended therapy

I need to kill
the malignant cells
proliferating, uncontrolled, in you.
If I don't hit hard and hit repeatedly,
the small remnants metastasized
to your remotest corners will recrudesce.
So, I need to be as ruthless as they are.

Just as a combo
of surgery, chemo, and radiation
is used to tackle tough cancers of the body,
I'll kill your abnormal cells with a persistent infusion
of nonjudgmental, real-time, self-remembering.
Mind, trust me, this blended therapy
will be a death blow to your spreading malignancy!

Traveling light

I am a radio that picks up signals,
a wire that transmits electricity

and a browser that navigates
and displays all the data

emerging from the various causes
and conditions of a moment.

But neither the new data
nor the old memories crush me

as I've learned to enable a lifeline button
called "auto-delete browsing history."

With this button on, it's become like a journey
through water, with no footprints left behind;

it's become like traveling light,
with no heavy baggage to carry.

With no tie around my neck

Took off my tie,
tossed my phone,
got out the door
and walked on.

Crossing Kathmandu's Ring Road,
I strode along a narrow trail
and soon reached a quiet place
filled with lots of trees and grace.

Leaving behind the rush and ado
of the polluted Kathmandu,
I got so much from that tiny trek
with no tie around my neck!

Lost and found

In a subtly cognizing infinite base,
faint humming vibrations arose
and breathing happened, in-out, in-out.
With the breathing, thoughts happened.

With the thoughts, the mind happened, the body happened,
I happened, others happened, and everything else happened.
And slowly, with all the gazillion proliferations,
the infinite base got lost.

When the loss was long and unbearable
and the longing intense,
the tool of awareness jump-started
and began to watch the breath.

With patient watching, thoughts began to subside,
and proliferations regress.
And gradually, with decades of incessant watching,
the base began to reappear.

It continues

This morning I was looking at the tree
my father had planted 50 years back.
Did I see the same tree living in his time?

Yes and no. Given that 99 percent
of a mature tree's cells are dead,
all the cells of his time must have died.

But I still saw the same essence in the tree
this morning that my father had seen then.
It continues, deathless!

Great Olympic moment

Ask a sportsperson
what it's like
to relax in action,
thoughtless,
during a great
Olympic moment.

Ask that Olympian
what it's like
to let go of the reigns
and let primal awareness
pop up and create
that wow moment.

Ask Mira Rai
what it's like
to be in an ultra running race
with the mind and the body
leaping ahead
in meditative silence.

The same dough dwells in them

The trillions of stars emit their individual lights,
but all those lights travel as one light
when they meet in the interstellar space.

The halibut, whales, and hippocampi
look and act differently but they all live
in the same ocean water.

Bagels, chapatis, croissants, and noodles
have their own shapes and tastes
but the same dough dwells in them.

Dear awareness, always help me see
the big similarities concealed
by the distracting superficial differences.

All there is, is seeing

Moments move. I don't.
I have no need to say
I'm new each moment.
I'm frozen, not in time, but out of it.
I'm stable, fixed, and fine.
I'm aloof, I'm final.

My senses are seeing, hearing, smelling, and touching
but they don't react.
They're at peace.
All there is, is seeing.
With all the happenings, nothing happens to me.
I'm unaffected, unshaken, aloof.

A strange state—no definitions, no boundaries, no worries.
Neither wanting nor not wanting.
Neither happy nor unhappy.
Neither existing nor not existing.
I'm aloof, I'm final.
All fine, all good, as is!

Beautiful at the borderline

It's beautiful to always be
at the borderline

between life and death,
where the two synergize

to create an ever fresh
experience

of living well and dying well
every single moment.

Every moment, the iced drink of death
cools off the heat of life

and the heart-warming soup of life
melts the ice of death.

It's beautiful to let
life and death cocreate

an awareness
that transcends them both.

Filling every alveolus of my lungs

I found wanting to take a deep, fulfilling breath
was the reason for a short breath.

The death of that wish
was what let a deep breath happen.

Trying to make life perfect, battling to keep things in order
brought me chaos and tension.

I didn't control the moment.
The moment controlled itself.

When I stepped aside and observed,
that's when I let the moment

work out its best
for itself and for me.

Ha! I finally saw that the death
of my wish for solutions was the solution.

With no wishes constricting my bronchi,
a deep breath happened,

filling all the alveoli of my lungs,
and oxygenating my being to see things as they are.

Just that, nothing more

I feel a waft of gentle breeze
touching my legs below my shorts
and the forearms below my t-shirt.
The unusually cool air for the end of June
brings back feelings of early spring.

A squirrel crossing the road
abruptly stops to check on me,
and equally abruptly races to reach
a maple tree on the side of the road.
A bird flies to my front from behind
and sits on a branch of the same tree.

It suddenly starts drizzling
and as I look up at the clouds,
fine raindrops stud my glasses,
creating a mysterious half-open,
half-closed experience of life.

I breathe easily with a soft smile
and walk on. I feel good and that's all.

Rising in spirals

I was sitting
by the window of my room
with a cup of hot tea
on a table in front of me.

I looked out.
It was calm and quiet.

As my eyes turned inwards,
I saw a cloud of steam
rise from the cup in spirals
and go out the window
up into the sky infinite,
leaving behind a fragrance
I loved.

Can't wait to reach home and sit again

This morning,
after a shower,
I sat to invoke my awareness,
who appeared
and blessed me with a good day.

But now in the evening,
driving back home,
I feel heavy, with my body sweaty
and my mind cluttered.
I can't wait to reach home

to take a second bath
and sit again with folded hands.
I know my awareness will pop back
to give me a peace-filled evening
and a sleep-filled night.

Looking up in freedom with hands outstretched

I recall an iconic scene of a movie
I saw long back.
How liberating it was!

Yes, I remember seeing that scene
in *Shawshank Redemption*
when Andy finally breaks out of the prison
he was condemned to for 19 long years
and looks up into the sky in freedom
with his hands outstretched.
Even though it was nighttime,
I remember clearly seeing
his liberated face lit up
with the flashes of lightening.

Andy is my inspiration.
I want to keep hoping
and working quietly, as he did.

I know one day I'll also look up
into the sky with outstretched hands,
freed from the prison of my own making.

I glimpsed You

I woke up, suddenly,
at dawn

and got
a fleeting glimpse of you.

What a lifetime chance
it was

to sneak a peek at you
during that rare moment

when my sleep had just ended
but thoughts hadn't arisen yet.

Sorry for what I've done to you

I've seen you
in many forms
and loved each of them.

I've seen you as ocean waves
splashing on the shore.
I've imagined you
rising from the sea
with the heat of the Sun
and heading towards my home,

and watched you fall
finally on my front yard
as the first rain of the summer,
exciting my olfactory nerves
to send your earth-mixed smell
to my brain's cortex.

I've heard you pour down
on the roof of my home
and overflow from the gutters,
prompting me to run out
and get wet with your Monsoon spirit.

I've seen you as Pokhara's Fewa Lake

reflecting on your chest
an inverted image of Annapurna
and as Virginia's Burke Lake
garlanded by fall trees.

How I've drunk you as water,
after every long walk,
cooling my esophagus,
and hydrating my cells!

I've seen you shine
as snow on the Himalaya
and flow down from there
to bless the land of Nepal
as Karnali, Gandaki, and Koshi.

But sadly, I've also seen your plight
as Bagmati below Pashupati.
I'm sorry for what I've done to you
for all that you've done for me!

What has life done?

Lost is the wood.
Only trees remain.

Lost is the canvas.
Only pictures remain.

Lost is the One Earth.
Only lines of the atlas remain.

Lost is the Valley of Kathmandu.
Only Bhaktapur, Kantipur, and Patan remain.

Lost is the landscape.
Only hills, mountains, and Himalayas remain.

Lost is the whole.
Only parts remain.

A sharp arrow

I couldn't dance
in the rains,
with happy blood
in my veins.

My ultramodern life

has pierced
my heart
like an arrow
from a bow.

I'm stuck where I am

A caterpillar afraid to morph
won't culminate in a butterfly.
A seed afraid to open up
won't germinate into a plant.

I'm blocking myself as a caterpillar
and locking myself as a seed,
missing the joys of a flying butterfly
and the thrills of a rising plant.

Slowly it is becoming clear,
metamorphosis is what I fear.
With no courage to change,
I'm stuck where I am.

Seriously! Are you dumb?

I met a strange guy with glitter in his eyes.
His body language seemed to indicate
he wanted to say something
he thought was important
but all I heard were a few cryptic sounds
that made no sense.

I also saw him repeatedly pointing
to the sky and beyond,
and cupping his hands behind his ears
and pulling them forward,
as if, funnily, asking me
to see the invisible and hear the inaudible.

I almost felt like saying,
"Seriously! Are you dumb?
I have no time for your crap
that I can't verify with my senses
and the methods and tools
of science I'm trained in."

Whose is all this?

A couple descending from a hike at Phulchoki Hill
looked at the mega-arc of a rainbow that appeared in the sky,

one end touching the Valley of Kathmandu
and the other dipping behind the summit of Shivapuri Hill.

Right then, thirteen chirping birds flew over the couple in a perfect V
and an airplane appeared far up in the sky.

A minute later, the couple resumed their descent in silence.
I was watching and marveling at all that panorama from a distance,

when I heard my own voice asking in silence, "Hello awareness, are you watching your own appearances?!"

Dear life!

Dear life,
I see you
always freak and fret.
Never see you
sit and rest.

Your toil and turmoil
led you nowhere.
Your theories and queries,
tools and techniques
gave no peace.

Still, I see you practice
breath-holding
and death postures,
making life
so very tough.

Can't you take
a little break
to live and laugh,
with breaths and postures
happening naturally?

Can you show me for once?

I feel your presence all the time
and keep imagining in millions of ways
you're possibly like this, you're possibly like that.

So near, yet so far. So real, yet so surreal.
You're like an invisible lover, pouring drinks all the time
and keeping me intoxicated but I can't quite hold you.

Can you show me for once what exactly you look like?
Or have you designed this mystery knowingly,
to keep the passion going, love flowing, endlessly?

Last night was strange

Last night was strange.
I couldn't remember my name
and many other things about me
despite my best efforts.

I was struggling hard to hold
whatever was remaining of myself,
when a final transition happened,
like a rocket escaping the earth's gravity.

With that leap, I became weightless.
My name, identity, and earnings
were no longer pulling me down.
I felt like a spaceship of awareness

moving without any frictions
arising from me and thee, mine and thine.
Indeed, last night was strange.
It was Ananda in annihilation.

Miles and miles

When A was available, I wanted B,
and when B was available, I wanted A.
Funny – when I got both, I craved C.

I always looked for something
other than what life was giving me
at each moment, at each stage, I was at.

Each time it was only a single moment missed
but when they all added up,
I found that I'd missed almost my entire life.

You're my two sides

You are the inhalation and exhalation of my lungs.
One coming in, expanding my chest
and the other going out, shrinking it.
With expansion, I become a playful universe.
With receding, I rest, slipping out of space-time.

You expand as awareness
and recede as death.
Both of you contain a tiny seed of the other,
cyclically giving rise to each other,
to keep me forever.

What would I do without the two of you –
how would I sustain myself,
alternating between play and rest?
I'm the coin and you're my two sides.
I love you both.

One flower to awareness and one to death

Tonight, at bedtime,
I'll offer one flower to awareness
and one to death,
asking them to work together
to wake me up tomorrow morning,
as a new flower,
fresh for the day,
freed of the dead past.

Every night, at bedtime,
I'll offer one flower to awareness
and one to death,
asking them to work together
to wake me up every morning
as an azure sky
without a cloud,
without limits.

***

ABOUT THE AUTHOR

Mohan Prasad Joshi, MD, MSc, MBBS

Dr. Joshi has over two decades of experience supporting 21 low- and middle-income countries in the technical implementation of antimicrobial resistance containment and other pharmaceutical systems strengthening activities through four U.S. Agency for International Development-funded global programs implemented by Management Sciences for Health in the United States. Before joining Management Sciences for Health, Dr. Joshi worked at Tribhuvan University's Institute of Medicine and Tribhuvan University Teaching Hospital in Nepal for nearly 20 years in various capacities, including as academic assistant dean, and professor and head of clinical pharmacology.

Dr. Joshi published a book of Nepali poems, *Kahaan Chha Thaaun* (Where Is the Place) in 2011 and was the lyricist for a Nepali audio album by the same name released in 2012.

YouTube Channel: https://www.youtube.com/@Dr.MohanPrasadJoshi

LinkedIn Profile: https://www.linkedin.com/in/mohan-p-joshi-md-msc-mbbs

ORCID ID: https://orcid.org/0000-0003-4846-6312

www.ingramcontent.com/pod-product-compliance
Lightning Source LLC
LaVergne TN
LVHW012025060526
838201LV00061B/4463